This was the year **Harry Truman** established America's leadership role in the postwar world. Outlining his Point Four program in his inaugural address, the president vowed to help European recovery through the Marshall Plan, give military aid to freedom-loving nations, support the UN, and share industrial and scientific progress with under-developed nations.

Under the Smith Act of 1940, 11 U.S. Communist Party leaders were found guilty of conspiracy to overthrow the government and were sentenced to prison.

IN PITTSBURGH, 480,000 UMW WORKERS WENT ON STRIKE IN SEPTEMBER. A MONTH LATER, 500,000 STEELWORKERS WALKED OFF THE JOB AND STAYED ON STRIKE FOR 42 DAYS.

THE PERMANENT HEADQUARTERS OF THE UNITED NATIONS WERE DEDICATED IN NEW YORK

YOU MUST REMEMBER THIS

1949

MILESTONES, MEMORIES,
TRIVIA AND FACTS, NEWS EVENTS,
PROMINENT PERSONALITIES &
SPORTS HIGHLIGHTS OF THE YEAR

TO :

FROM :

MESSAGE :

selected and researched
by
betsy dexter

WARNER  TREASURES ™

PUBLISHED BY WARNER BOOKS

A TIME WARNER COMPANY

Warner Books, Inc.
1271 Avenue of the Americas
New York, New York 10020

Warner Treasures is a
trademark of Warner Books, Inc.

A Time Warner Company

DESIGN:
CAROL BOKUNIEWICZ DESIGN
PRINTED IN SINGAPORE
FIRST PRINTING : SEPTEMBER 1995
10 9 8 7 6 5 4 3 2 1
ISBN: 0-446-91083-X

PRESIDENT TRUMAN RAISED THE MINIMUM WAGE FROM 40 TO 74 CENTS AN HOUR.

The senate ratified an agreement establishing **NATO**, the North Atlantic Treaty Organization. On August 24, President Truman signed the treaty.

After a year of record profits, GM voted to pay out $190 million—the biggest dividend in U.S. business history.

newsreel

Alger Hiss was tried on two counts of perjury about his dealings with Whittaker Chambers. The trial resulted in a 8-4 hung jury, and another trial was scheduled.

ALGER HISS

**IN SOUTH AFRICA, THE GOVERN-
MENT PASSED A LAW MAKING
MARRIAGE BETWEEN BLACKS
AND WHITES ILLEGAL.**

international

headlines

Russian-controlled East Germany declared itself the **German Democratic Republic**. West Germany established itself as the Federal Republic of Germany, with Konrad Adenauer as chancellor.

On September 23, President Truman announced that the Soviets had exploded an atom bomb. The weapon was developed by a team of physicists including Andrei Sakharov and German Nobel laureate Gustav Hertz.

IN CHINA,

the Communist Chinese drove the
Nationalists off the Mainland. The
People's Republic of China was
proclaimed on October 1, with
Mao Tse-tung as chairman.
Chiang Kai-shek estab-
lished his Nationalist
government on the
former island of
Formosa, now
called Taiwan.

Ezra Pound, under indictment for treason and in a Washington, DC, mental hospital, won the $1,000 Bollingen Prize for poetry for *The Pisan Cantos*.

Louis Armstrong won the hearts of Frenchmen, teaching Parisians to speak "le jazz" as he and his band performed to standing ovations.

On January 19, Congress decided to raise the presidential salary to $100,000, with $50,000 in expenses.

cultural
milestones

IN LONDON, ADVERTISING LIGHTS
WENT ON AFTER A 10-YEAR RESTRICTION.

On September 30, the Berlin airlift was halted after 277,264 flights.

On July 13, the Vatican, under the personal direction of Pope Pius XII, declared its intention to ex-communicate Communists.

The ENOLA GAY, the plane that dropped the A-bomb on Hiroshima, was presented to the Smithsonian Museum.

ARCHITECT PHILIP JOHNSON DESIGNED HIS FAMOUS GLASS HOUSE, IN NEW CANAAN, CT. THE HOUSE WAS COMPLETELY TRANSPARENT EXCEPT FOR A SOLID COLUMN CONTAINING THE BATHROOM.

HARVARD LAW SCHOOL AGREED TO BEGIN ADMITTING WOMEN ON OCTOBER 9.

7

ON JULY 7, JACK WEBB PREMIERED IN "DRAGNET," DRAMATIZING REAL-LIFE POLICE CASES.

radio

NEWSPAPER CRITICS' RADIO CHAMPIONS OF 1949

Champion of Champions **Jack Benny, Bing Crosby**

Comedian **Jack Benny, Bob Hope, Henry Morgan**

Comedienne **Eve Arden, Joan Davis, Marie Wilson**

Comedy Team **Fibber McGee and Molly, Dean Martin and Jerry Lewis, Burns and Allen**

Best Master of Ceremonies **Bing Crosby, Arthur Godfrey, and Groucho Marx**

Daytime Program **Arthur Godfrey, Fred Waring**

Quiz Show **"You Bet Your Life," "Twenty Questions," "Sing It Again," "Who Said That?"**

Audience Participation Program **"Truth or Consequences," "People Are Funny," "Stop the Music"**

Mystery Show **"Suspense," "Adventures of Sam Spade," "Dragnet"**

On February 12, in Ecuador, a mob burned down a radio station after a broadcast of H. G. Wells's "The War of the Worlds."

8

In January, NBC unveiled TV's first daytime soap opera, "These Are My Children." The show used blackboards as cue cards, giving performers a far-away look in their eyes as they strained to read their lines.

On January 12, "KUKLA, FRAN AND OLLIE" arrived on NBC.

television

On August 25, RCA announced the invention of a system for broadcasting color TV.

On January 21, the first **Emmy Awards** were handed out by Walter O'Keefe at the Hollywood Athletic Club. **"Pantomime Quiz,"** a local Los Angeles show, was named Most Popular TV Show.

On May 5, Arlene Francis transferred her successful radio game show, **"Blind Date,"** to ABC. Anxious bachelors, hoping to be picked for a night out, took turns trying to woo a model hidden from sight by a studio wall.

In March, ABC brought the violent cheesecake of Roller Derby to the air. Ken Nydell did the skate-by-skate description as healthy young women threw blocks and roundhouses at their buxom opponents.

science

On December 26, **Albert Einstein** put forth his new generalized theory of gravitation, which attempted to unite the major forces of nature in one unified intellectual concept.

Linus Pauling discovered the molecular flaw responsible for sickle-cell anemia, the debilitating blood disease primarily affecting Black Americans.

AN AMERICAN B-50 BOMBER, LUCKY LADY II, COMPLETED THE FIRST NONSTOP FLIGHT AROUND THE WORLD.

The **Nobel Prize** was shared by Swiss physiologist Walter Rudolf Hess, for his work in determining the functions of different brain parts, and neurosurgeon Antonio Egas Moniz, of Portugal, for development of the prefrontal lobotomy—a radical brain operation performed on mentally ill patients.

The American Cancer Society and National Cancer Institute warned this year that cigarette smoking could cause cancer.

On May 27, actress Rita Hayworth, on the rebound from ex-hubby Orson Welles, married Moslem playboy Aly Khan.

DEATHS

Maurice Maeterlinck, Belgian poet and playwright, died on May 6.
Margaret Mitchell, 49, *Gone With the Wind* author, died on August 16 after being struck by a speeding car in Atlanta.
Bill "Bojangles" Robinson, 70, the world's greatest tap dancer, died on November 25. Besides starring in Broadway and moving pictures, Robinson also held the world record in running backward.

births

Jessica Lange, movie star, Cloquet, MN, April 20.

Patti LuPone, actress, Northport, NY, April 21.

Billy Joel, singer-songwriter, Bronx, NY, May 9.

Hank Williams, Jr., country music star, Shreveport, LA, May 26.

Meryl Streep, actress, Summit, NJ, June 22.

Shelley Duvall, actress, Houston, July 7.

Rick Springfield, pop star, Sydney, Australia, August 23.

Gene Simmons, KISS founder, Haifa, Israel, August 25.

Ed Begley, Jr., actor, September 16, in Los Angeles.

Bruce Springsteen, rock star, Freehold, NJ, September 23.

milestones

Solomon Guggenheim, 88, millionaire industrialist and founder of the Guggenheim Museum of Modern Art in New York City, died on November 3.

Sigourney Weaver, actress, New York City, October 8.

Bonnie Raitt, blues singer, Burbank, CA, November 8.

Gary Shandling, comic, Tucson, AZ, November 29.

Jeff Bridges, actor, Los Angeles, December 4.

Sissy Spacek, actress, Quitman, TX, December 25.

11

lovesick blues Hank Williams and His Drifting Cowboys

mule train Frankie Laine

i've got a lovely bunch of cocoanuts Merv Griffin, with Freddy Martin and His Orchestra

candy kisses George Morgan

baby, it's cold outside Esther Williams and Ricardo Montalban

i'm dreamin' with my eyes wide open Patti Page

i yust go nuts at christmas Yogi Yorgesson and the John Duffy Trio

most popular vocalists:

Perry Como

Bing Crosby

Doris Day

Dinah Shore

Frank Sinatra

Jo Stafford

hit music

most popular dance bands:

Guy Lombardo

Vaughn Monroe

Les Brown

The runaway novelty smash of the season was **"Rudolph, the Red-Nosed Reindeer,"** the holiday hit by songwriter Johnny Marks.

Fearing its "suggestive" message, radio censors moved to keep **"Baby, It's Cold Outside"** off the airwaves for most of 1949.

HANK WILLIAMS

13

canasta fever swept the United States this year, as evidenced in the 3 guaranteed game-helpers gracing the bestseller list.

bestselling

nonfiction

1. **white collar zoo**
   clare barnes, jr.

2. **how to win at canasta**
   oswald jacoby

3. **the seven-storey mountain**
   thomas merton

4. **home sweet zoo**
   clare barnes, jr.

5. **cheaper by the dozen**
   frank b. gilbreth, jr., and ernestine gilbreth carey

6. **the greatest story ever told**
   fulton oursler

7. **canasta, the argentine rummy game**
   ottilie h. reilly and alexander rosa

8. **canasta**
   artayeta de viel

9. **peace of soul**
   fulton j. sheen

10. **a guide to confident living**
    norman vincent peale

GEORGE ORWELL'S

1984, published this year, foresaw a grim future of censorship, paranoia, and life dominated by Big Brother totalitarian government.

French author Simone de Beauvoir published her feminist treatise

the second sex

books

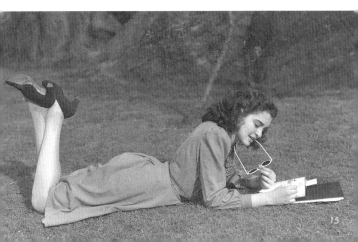

fiction

1. **the egyptian**
   mika waltari

2. **the big fisherman**
   lloyd c. douglas

3. **mary**
   sholem asch

4. **a rage to live**
   john o'hara

5. **point of no return**
   john p. marquand

6. **dinner at antoine's**
   frances parkinson keys

7. **high towers**
   thomas b. costain

8. **cutlass empire**
   van wyck mason

9. **pride's castle**
   frank yerby

10. **father of the bride**
    edward streeter

nobel prize
William Faulkner

pulitzer prize
Arthur Miller for
Death of a Salesman

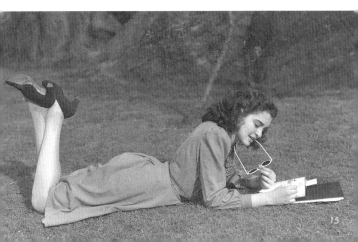

15

In 2 title fights this year, Jake LaMotta KOd Marcel Cerdan to capture the middleweight crown. In the heavy-weight category, Ezzard Charles took the title in a decision over Jersey Joe Walcott.

Joe Louis, the Brown Bomber, quit the ring after 11 years as heavyweight champ. Son of a sharecropper who died when Louis was 4, he started boxing at 18. He defended the title 25 times.

IN AUTO RACING, BILL HOLLAND WON THE INDY 500, AVERAGING 126.244 MPH IN A BLUE CROWN SPECIAL RACER.

The Yankees gave Joe DiMaggio a $90,000 salary this year, making him the highest-paid player in baseball.

sports

In baseball, though the Yankees defeated the Brooklyn Dodgers in the World Series, Dodger Jackie Robinson, named Most Valuable Player in the National League, batted .342 in the 1949 season, to lead the league.

In pro football, the Philadelphia Eagles shut out the Rams, 14–0, to take their 2nd straight title.

Hepburn and Tracy were reunited this year in *Adam's Rib*. After *Woman of the Year*, Hepburn and Tracy made three "battle of sexes" films.

Victor Mature, 1949's hunk of the year, was enlisted to play Samson in Cecil B. DeMille's toga-tugger **Samson and Delilah.** This film helped kick off a round of sword-and-sandal spectaculars.

oscar winners

Best Picture **All the King's Men,** Rossen / Columbia, produced by *Robert Rossen.* Best Actor **Broderick Crawford,** *All the King's Men.* Best Actress **Olivia De Havilland,** *The Heiress.* Best Supporting Actor **Dean Jagger,** *Twelve O'Clock High.* Best Supporting Actress **Mercedes Mc-Cambridge,** *All the King's Men.* Best Director **Joseph L. Mankiewicz,** *A Letter to Three Wives.* Best Original Screenplay **The Stratton Story,** *Douglas Morrow.* Best Adapted Screenplay **A Letter to Three Wives,** *Joseph L. Mankiewicz.*